Oily and the Flood

by Christopher Awdry

Illustrated by Marc Vyvyan-Jones

Day after day the engines listened to the rain drumming on the roof of the shed. Because of it no visitors had come to the park for some time.

SOUTHERN
Western
Eastbourne
Rachel
General
3802

Mr Mike and Mr Luke wore things they called wellingtons—they seemed to have had them on for days.

"The water in the lake is rising," Mr Mike told the engines. "We may have to move you to somewhere dry."

But the rain didn't stop.

"Where can we go?" the engines asked anxiously next morning.

Mr Mike shook his head. Just then, Mr Luke came in.

"The boat has drifted away," he said. "I can see it on the other side of the lake."

Mr Mike and Mr Luke squelched round the lake together. They found that they couldn't get near the boat because that part of the railway was under water.

The front of the boat had caught under a fence.

"If the water rises any more," said Mr Luke, "the boat might tip over. We must get it loose, but how?

They shook their heads and trudged wetly back to the station.

"We could reach it if we had another boat," said Mr Mike. "Or you could swim out to it."

Mr Luke made it clear what he thought of that!

Brittannia
Ayrshire Yeomanry
Eastbourne Herald
orm 2
D 7042
1H12

Then Mr Luke had an idea. He went into the shed and pressed the starter of Oily, whose proper name, as I'm sure you'll remember, is *Eastbourne Herald*.

"What are you doing?" the other engines asked.

"Going to rescue the boat," said Mr Luke. "It's where Rachel found the goose, and the line is flooded."

"But..." quavered Oily, "if the line is flooded, I shall get water in my works, and..."

"You won't," said Mr Luke. "Wait and see."

He coupled Oily to some coaches.

"That's the wrong end," said the coaches. "You're at the back, not the front."

"Wait and see," said Mr Luke again.

Carefully Oily pushed the coaches round the line. Mr Luke rode on the coaches at the front, while Mr Mike rode on the engine.

When they reached the place, Oily carefully pushed the coaches into the water. The coaches shivered as the water crept up their wheels.

Mr Luke, in front, was careful to keep his feet dry. The coaches squeaked anxiously, but were determined to be brave, because they wanted to help.

At last the first coach reached the boat and, skilfully, Mr Luke scrambled into it. The boat rocked, but Mr Luke steadied it by holding on to the fence.

Then Mr Mike reversed Oily, and drew the coaches safely back to the station. They were given a good clean and oiling before being put away in their shed.

Oily never knew if they discovered that he hadn't even got his wheels wet! He certainly never told them.

That night in the engine shed Oily became a hero too.

"Fancy going out in all that weather!" the other engines said. "How brave!"